THE BURNING PLACE

poems by

Judith Bishop

Fithian Press   Santa Barbara   1994

The author wishes to thank the editors of the following publications in which some of these poems first appeared: *Kalliope, Book of Contemporary Myth, Miwok Archaeological Preserve of Marin (MAPOM) News, Taos Review, Living Spirit, Sri Chinmoy Award, Santa Barbara Independent, Shots, Bulletin of Primitive Technology, Mildred, Queen of Swords Press, Stone Country.*

Some of these poems first appeared in the chapbook *The Longest Light* published by *Five Fingers Review*, San Francisco, 1991.

FIRST EDITION

Designed by Judith Bishop
Cover photograph by Judith Bishop
Author photograph by Brian Tramontana

Published by Fithian Press
A Division of Daniel and Daniel, Publishers, Inc.
Post Office Box 1525
Santa Barbara, CA 93102

Library of Congress Cataloguing-in-Publication Data

Bishop, Judith
    The burning place : poems / by Judith Bishop —1st ed.
         p. cm.
    ISBN 1-56474-110-9
    1. Indians of North America—Poetry. 2. Women—United States—Poetry.
    3. Nature—Poetry.   I. Title.
    PS3552.I7714B87   1994
    811'.54—dc20   94-12622
                                  CIP

This book is dedicated to Laughing Coyote

and to the memory of William Dickey.

CONTENTS

I – THE BURNING PLACE

THE BURNING PLACE

A hundred Shoshone could live here
on spring water, pine nuts, mesquite pods,
jackrabbits, lizards,
and the minute grass seeds.
When the whites crowded in
it became death valley.
The earlier people had patience.
A stunning sun burned away the rest.

It burns my murderous whiteness
until I become darker,
thoughtful, more deliberate,
more careful where I step.
In the dunes before dawn
there are tracks like stitches
between the holes under the creosote bushes.
The kangaroo rats have switched their tails
and beetles made prints like zippers.
Where the raven hunted that night
I begin to find something.

The camera is mechanical
but so was the long, hooked stick
that pulled chuckwallas from their holes.
As a full moon sets the sun rises
and the dunes balance,
every lighted surface given its shadow.

THE RELEVANCE OF TECHNIQUE

Take the colors down
print them
down, down,
till they are subtle as sage,
transparent as sand.
A breathing lightness
is where the spirit lives,
for a thousand years,
and now.
Land's ancestors
tell me the secret,
for we're almost dead.
The Hopi prophecies
are truer than newspapers.
Match the desert,
the real colors,
get subtle enough,
not brighter than life.
We dissolve in exaggeration,
clouds eat us up, water
runs off, too many trees go down,
down, down.
Take the colors down,
even to boredom,
the color of organs in the body.

THE BODY OF THE LAND

Chaco Canyon

The body of the land,
breath shimmering at noon,
held after sundown,
moving a little, like sleep, with stars.
The edge of the mesa's lifted hip,
the long wash, spine of the canyon,
as white as vertebrae, its cracked mud
neat bones fitted together.
It cannot get up and walk away.

In the early afternoon
I go to sleep on a rock slab
and its contours fit my bones,
its thoughts are mine
and my body is its other side.
When my child, years ago,
snugged against me, mouth around breast,
elbows and knees tucked in, hands
clinging like starfish,
perhaps we were as close as we are to the earth.
When the breeze stops, the heat
bakes me like a pot.

Anasazi came here because it was hard
and they would not forget to pray.
I leave leaves of sage
under stone chips, secretly
pour my heart into the ground.
At the center of the canyon
Fajada Butte lifts up its calendar,
a spiral behind three slices of stone
that focus daggers of light
at the height of solstice, equinox,
and the apogee of the moon.
This is the navel of life
and the only schedule for survival.

MYSTERY

This early, the shape of the bush isn't clear.
Perhaps it is a bear, an ally,
whose shoulder I search out,
or else it is creosote
whose roots hold small animals together.
Morning is confusion, mists
of smells rise with the light.
The very stones tell of themselves,
their molecules moving like tongues.
They wince and move over under my feet.
There is nowhere I can move that I don't rearrange,
this is why I got up early.
I thought it was to catch the undisturbed light,
but more truthfully, it is to pray,
to get down on my bones in the growth
and bow until I'm invisible.
For if I say a word, things will change,
the rocks could roll away, sticks
break, and I be faced with my power
as I was with the mountain lion
whose lair I had looked for for months
on the back trails near piles of bones
stripped out of the deer
but she was not there. She
crossed my path like the grass walking.
She was not afraid and I was astounded,
her tan color melding into gray
as the wild oats decayed down through summer.
She was the exact color of her surroundings
and had command of them.
I did not breathe, she was my breath,
and now it comes back.
In moments the sun will lift,
or rather the mountain's edge turn
under it and push it up into the day.
The earth gives me the sun
and these thoughts, these prayers
come from the bones.

MEETING

I

Never have I walked so lightly,
a pebble's height
above the packed clay path
up around the pond.
The ocean and its traffic fall away.
Woodmint, hemlock, yarrow,
the practical flowers,
brush my knees, a yellow lupine
full of bees, softly
lets me walk through it.
The trail is as old as the tribes
and I pay attention
to the goldfinch on the briar
and to rabbit who appears and vanishes at my feet.

Past the poison oak
the hilltop and all the long marsh
fill the horizon.
Aloneness is like the light wind.
I search several ways down,
first through the bracken
and pick up the way in deep sand,
pocked and tumbled
through two dunes
so overcast with spring flowers
– red and orange and purple –
I suddenly sit down, in paradise.
Where the roots have been walked on
they are bare and snaky.
There is no more to know
of any consequence.

II

Further on the hemlocks close in
and along the estuary I think I'm invisible
until a green turtle hurries underwater
and the other one swings its neck.
The sky is full of white flowers

and the mound is ahead,
a dome of grassed over oyster shells
deep in the waterways and reeds.
I halt in the blackberries.
The way opens up
to a grove of spotted trees
that hang to the water and rustle.

Going back the long way
I cross the road to the ocean,
run easily on the wet sand
as the gray surf arches in,
and pick up two talking feathers.
The winds are cold and wet.
At the car I shake sand from my shoes
and drive to the restaurant.
Two friends in beautiful red shirts
sweep in and bring you.
The feathers on your arm
are redtailed hawk and peregrine.
I tell you that at Mono Lake I heard your ancestors
and have listened ever since.

COYOTE HILL

The upland plover
calls over the industrial park,
calls into the sulfurous heat
of early September.
My hot, summer skin is so happy
it almost opens its mouth.
This morning, my period.
For a few days I'm without you,
returned to this land.
I am a great yellow field
that you sow and tend and harvest
but today I rest in my furrows,
thick heat a shawl over my head.
Tonight the moon will be over half full
and I would like other women with me.
When the moon is perfectly full
again I'll be stripling,
strong, thin, older woman.
Then we can run like coyotes
catching mice in the cool light,
zigzagging over fields
hunting to discover
what nourishes us.
The answer may dive into its hole.
We'll sit down patiently.
Or when the moon is stripped and new
again we'll startle each other in the dark.
You have brought me around,
like the bird's cry,
into the deepest cycle.

THE BURNING MAN

It is not what I feel about us
that interests you.
There is something more urgent,
this hot wind in the grasses,
the seeds, detached, that burrow;
writing, your relation to it.

You bury it all
in notebooks, show no one.
What can the native say
that hasn't been used against them?

Perhaps it will flame up,
sweep through the canyons, burn down the cover
that's hidden the real nature of things.

It may burn out your soul,
your great luminous eyes
go dry and irritated in the smoke.
Fires are part of a cycle
so huge we cannot see it.
What will not grow without it?
What plant, animal? Survival?

Over some time
I have been learning
how to tear myself open
and withstand what happens.
You may come to speak for a whole people
and that makes you more vulnerable.

In New England, after a burn,
the maple, birch, and poplar come in,
their broad leaves shelter
for pine and spruce, deep seedlings.

Here in the West there are few meadows
where things happen so gently.
The vast fires desolate,
for years only stones and scorpions
hold the ground.
                    Tonight
the air is sweet and cool.
Let's talk like the evening wind,
softly, about what happens.

WHERE THE EAGLES ARE

I bring my shadow into line
with the thin white oak
and feel drawn in,
cool my injured foot,
and write.
After a drink of water,
after cheese and bread,
I have lain poured out into the sun
among small, white rocks
on this high place.
Grandfather
whom I never saw,
who has set my course,
blanketed me in light.
My body filled in the uneven earth
and I let go into her
and for a while slept deeper than beds.
About two o'clock the birds began,
warbler, woodpeckers, a conversation of crows,
the warbler's small voice precise.

We had come up the hill slowly
but had found feathers
as we found Medicine all this day.
The first feather was at his feet
and he breathed "Ho."
We had heard the whistles
and looked up. Two adult bald eagles
spiraled above us, a young one
following first one then the other
as they taught it to fly.
Hundreds of feet above the water
it had flown above the mother,
bumped into her, backed off.
She made a perfect roll
end to end of her extended black wings.
The young one tried
but came only half way around.
Again the eagle spun like a slow propeller
and then swiveled her head back
watching the young one.
The young eagle was last to go,
cruising back and forth below us,
its back feathers mottled.

We offered tobacco.
I didn't dare watch him pray.
That morning he bought me coffee
with his last dollar
without thinking, as I would for him.
He is of the eagle clan
and the only person
I have ever completely listened to.

He's left me
to hunt further.
These are his hills, his eagles,
though his tribe is near the Sierras.
Alone, I set four white stones
and one in the center.
It is four o'clock now
and the crows begin again,
insistently. The warbler
has become a cedar flute.
The tiny grass stems
curve into four o'clock light,
and the littlest hopping spider
has left my foot for the south rock,
that direction we all go towards.

This morning at about seven,
as I'd driven the mountains,
the dawn was breakfast fire
stirred out of the ashes,
the light dirty and slow
until the sun, like a live coal,
rolled over the edge
and the rest of the horizon
along bitten peaks and ridges
transformed
into light so itself there was no color.
At the end of this day
the fire is banked
and we drive
into a great dark furnace
where scattered street lights,
or a few farms, are embers,
planets and stars
patterns around the iron door.
We are the burning,
our anguish never stops.

FIRST SWEAT

Nine women, nine men
circle the fire where forty stones heat
in a volcano under the logs.
We are wrapped in bright towels
and I bind my uneasiness.
The firekeeper passes a square drum,
pouches of herbs, a large feather, antlers,
down the dark doorway.
"All my relations."
The leader's arm reaches out for them
and we wind clockwise
out of the sunlight, down into the lodge
with him, snug ourselves against the cool dirt walls,
knees drawn up in a tight circle.
A pit in the center, the rock's nest, is still empty
and I feel hollow, afraid,
though you are at my right shoulder.

The keeper brings in the Pipe and the tamper
and the leader fills the redstone bowl,
returns it to him to go on the outside altar.
A bucket of water with a large gourd is lowered
and then the rocks,
one by one on a pitchfork, the ash blown off,
until there is a new volcano
at the heart of us. Each person offers herbs
to the stones and I try not to cough in the small smoke.
You spread its comfort with your feather
and some waft it into themselves with their hands.
The blessing is begun and the door is closed,
the edge of heavy quilts
that cover the saplings arched over us
is pulled down and we are in the dark.
Mother earth, protect us now,
do not let me panic in this closeness
and darkness and heat and smoke,
let me join the suffering of the world,
not try to escape it.

I hear the first gourd of water
dance on stone, and heavy hot steam
comes up over my knees
and tries to go in my nose.
I will not let it in me to scald

and fight it, panic rising. Out. Out.
We begin to sing the Pipe Filling Song
and it pulls the breath through me,
wet and bearable. I relax a little
though my heart is still echoing.
Is it strong enough? The song continues
and the leader dedicates us
to the North and to birth and to infancy.
I know nothing except that I'm alive
and there are others with me.
The woman on my left falters
and I try to steady her with my body,
soothe her with my arm and hand.
I feel stronger, and the door is flung open.
Light, very far away, across the circle,
and I do not have to run into it.

The woman asks the leader the first question
– what if we faint? Ignore
the mind's clamors and pay attention
to your real state. Let
everything pass through. Faint if you want to,
there's no harm.
More water, new rocks, redder now,
and the door goes down.
After the Children's Song and prayer for the East,
the men begin their prayers, one by one,
remember, by name, all their relations.
Gratitude pours out with the sweat,
the body's tears, and tears
fall like water on the rocks.

The last man, after you pray for your family,
you pray for the artists.
This has been very long, my heart
knocks insistently
and the door flies up and light and air come in.
A few leave, the pressure is hard,
and prayers go with them, and wistfulness.
This time the gourd of water goes around.
I take only one swallow
and that mouthful of water is sweet.
We sing the Curing Song, towards the South,
adulthood, being in the middle,
and I begin the women's prayers.
I sing a thanks song
but in a very small, strange voice, like an echo.

Still, everyone says Ho.
I go through my family
praying for each difficult one, thanking
them for life itself.
Thanks comes as a relief.
Letting go the resentments,
I rise in my heart as one feels
taking off a huge pack after the climb.
And one by one the women
– faster than the men –
pray and thank and let go. One
has to leave, calls, All My Relations,
and the flap rises and we leave it there.
The Pipe is brought in, lit fitfully,
and one by one we smoke, as each
had prayed. I still don't understand it
except that the smoke rises like the spirit.
The door closes after the last rocks,
now huge and fiery,
settle in their herbs.
We sing the Willow Song. I know it,
I am almost comfortable,
a dangerous feeling in ceremony,
and we are dedicated to the West,
old age, and death that moves on.

Do we become spirits, Grandfather? How?
I've never believed this before
but held in Mother Earth, enduring
the breath of the rocks, oldest ancestors,
praying as the leader prayed now
for the world's pain and endurance,
something opens in me.
As he asks the blessing again
from all our relations
the door opens into the sun.

II – THE LONGEST LIGHT

IN THE TULES

Deep in the rushes,
cutting them one by one,
emerald stems slippery white at the base,
I hear only rustling,
my own and the fiery dragonflies
red as knife cuts, mating.
Tules, smooth as whips,
pile in bundles for a house.
If I lived this deep and slow
I'd give up freedom.
Two small snakes with white stripes
swim with their mouths open
like purse seines,
purple pennyroyal bristling
on a bank rich with bees.

BASKETS
for Susan Billy

I – Sedge

There is a knot in the center,
at the beginning,
a twist
that then winds up into a rim,
begins to coil, a willow
inserted in the heart.

After cedar smudge and prayer
I walk up a bank
and stop where my feet buzz,
dig immediately to the first one.
Ah, Mother, you are kind,
you spoil me with another,
and then one longer than a yard,
because we prayed for something special.
I burrow from my knees,
ass up, arms intent, scratched
from the triangular, silicate leaves
perhaps as old as horsetails.
The roots run from clump to clump of the grasses,
my fingers digging, following the yard
of furry, skin-like brown,
thick as pencils,
sketching a great web
through this sandy soil
loosened for a thousand years
by your Grandmothers.
Tunneling from one to the next
I mole after them,
leave mounds.
O when it rains
may all this go smooth again,
I am not Indian enough
to cover all my tracks.
Looking up, over the bent leaves,
women's backs, rounded,
solid as rocks,
my friends, my relations.
When I bring up the roots,
lay them on my purple towel,

there is no dirt on them,
they are clean as spider legs.
We gather to eat
on blankets in a gully,
our foods go around with the talk
of massacre and menopause.
Easily we share
what is desperate alone.
If we had years together,
weaving, how solid we'd be.
Folding the meal away
we split the roots, neatly,
with teeth and fingers,
then skin them
to a thin, tough core.

II – Willows

The leaves are soft as animals,
thin and silver furred,
rustling,
their songs like love songs.
To be right for baskets
the bushes need cutting back
which often the highway crews do
but then they spray them.
Here they're way down the bank
by the creek
and we scramble
through burrs and thistles.
A pickup from the Rancheria
careens the curve above,
cursing our whiteness.
I bring home two shoots
and stick them in the ground
near the hose faucet.
Materials here,
in a suburban yard?
Baskets come from the magic woods
but also from my white hands.

III – Redbud

And then there is contrast,
the dark of design. Holding the stick in my teeth
my thumbs split it into three,
and then I split each down
to a woody bark strip,
red-brown, lithe.
A man taught me to do this
and as I go on with this art I miss him.
The strips have to be shaved
thin as sedge.
They, too, season for a year.
Time is nothing,
how we do things, a life.
The gathering is hard,
preparation careful as breath.
Foremost is patience,
to wait for the truth of things.

IV – Weaving

Under a ramada of brown branches
a dozen women concentrate
until their hands become knowledgeable
as they were for thousands of years.
The singer sings to us,
his clapper's beat our hearts',
and the bead makers join,
the talk widening.
Perhaps this is all pretend,
the village, after all,
is a reconstruction
and no one actually lives here
but on the days we gather
we live here.
If the redbud and the sedge
are pulled snug enough
around three willow rods
baskets can hold water.
Sedge white as my skin,
redbud rich as yours,
binds round stitch by stitch,
coils in a rising spiral
woven from ourselves
– to store things in,
cook with, carry our burdens.

MARSH MOON

Foam floats on the river
like the moon in darkness.
Water murmurs
and I walk out on its bank
my pockets full of prayers.
What awful sorrow have I forgotten!
Grandmother moon, slim
as a girl or the very old,
stringent, you remember everyone.
After all the ducks have fled
I stop in the dark,
hunch down among the pickleweed
and dig in tobacco ties –
pleas and requests and gratitude.
When I step the dirt down
my offering is invisible.
I turn to all the directions,
touch the earth once more.
Two cinnamon teal scale down,
curved as eyelashes.
Dark moon, you are stuffed into your bright cap
like the acorns that fed the tribes
who lived by these marshes.
Their murder is the sorrow above all others.

THE MEDICINE WHEEL
for Sukuyb'Tet

The snow cleaned air
glitters between the boughs.
Jack Stone brings a magnificent pole
the bugs have numbered and written on,
and we tie on our hoop
of willow, feathers, stones, and prayer ties,
bear its colorfulness through woods to the circle,
set it at the center fire
next to our stone.
From there granite rocks spoke out
to each direction,
circle you
who lead, direct, pray.
The women are in blanket skirts
and the fringes blow a little
above their boots;
all the men are with us.
We are ready to recreate the world.
I have come over half a century to this place.
Snow, sun, rain, skirmish
and the pines glisten.
The drums and rattles begin.

Great Mystery,
sun and center,
fire of life,
maker of molecules,
thank you for this good day,
for our lives.

I stand at the West where prayer
begins its directions, towards sunset,
reaching deep, inward,
as though only understanding our pain,
our death, teaches us how to live.
Here the bear,
obsidian, black eagles,
send out waters, herbs, Medicine,
the care of life
that comes of self knowledge.

The drums beat their pattern six times
and we turn to the North,
to White Buffalo Calf Woman, bald eagles,
the great trees, night, the red Pipe,
sources of vision,

the magic that comes of great age –
perspective.
You are so eloquent
I am breathless,
no longer know who'se praying,
all of us sounding in your voice.

To the East a cloth on the ground
holds instruments
and the blessing feathers.
Over them you invoke
the spiritual life, that seed
from which everything comes,
direction of sunrise.

Towards the South your grandson
sits, dreams in his eyes.
Here our physical lives
work themselves out,
our childhood,
loves, children,
lessons.
All the rest
is beyond this innocence.

And now we lean into the ground,
your prayers pour like the waters,
most of us are crying
for all the injuries,
the imperilment of the ground we stand on.
O Mother Earth forgive us,
we've come to learn how to live,
how to continue.
Does anyone beyond this clearing
hear? Those who, thirsty, waste the waters,
hungry, waste the land, houseless,
bring down the trees? Those on their backs?
If we hear, the enormous power of the earth
will transmit to everyone.

MAKING STRING

from milkweed, hemp, nettles.
In the sun with others, hands working,
I scrape dry stalks
till the life glue flakes off,
crack the canes lengthways
– grass bones – slit them down,
roll them flat open to the marrow,
and snap knuckle lengths
over my left fingers,
pull out handfuls of floss.
I twist a half till a loop twists up,
roll each end along the thigh,
rolling the two strands
side by side under the palm
till they spring back wound,
splice in new fiber.
I run the line through flame,
skin the whiskers.
This string is strong
for snares or for tying together.

THE VILLAGE

As I come away my hands still smell of venison.
The sweet fat didn't wash away under the water tap. I had unwrapped
the meat from parchment and foil as it came from the fire pit
and cut it up for people to eat. And this was my animal,
my guide, guardian of my journeys, friend of my dreams.
Swift, intelligent animal, forgive me.

All day the sun had been bright and cool. People
went about the booths of rattles, jewelry, clappers, feathers,
talking slowly. So much smiling. Big time.
There were many white visitors. They tasted
the fry bread, smiled shyly, and lingered
under ramadas made of willow and feathery redwood branches.
Their children darted into tule and bark cochas
pretending they lived there, squatted in the coolness, and darted out.

Late, a close crowd of Pomo, Miwok and friends remained.
Most knew most by name. A few prepared the dishes.
A man took the spirit plate to the fire,
offered food to each direction till it was gone.
One who was miraculously just out of jail
gave the blessing, that we always be free to gather like this.
The elders lined up first, and the dancers. I took my plate
to sit with a drum maker and the jeweler's mother. Her son
and the grandchildren joined and we ate, told stories, joked in a soft way.

When the deer was bones, the grandmother
said they used to take them back into the woods. The sky darkens
and we gather logs, bales, blankets around the dance ground.
The medicine person's wife stokes the center fire
and the semicircle of singers clack the clapper sticks into their hands.
Five or six boys come out of the dark in feather kilts, feather horns,
their torsos copper in the firelight.
Bear, otter, bird – songs spin them around the fire.
Girls on either side sway under their abalone pendants.
There is one man, heavy and graceful,
his feathers barred gray, a child with him
in small regalia, dancing a dance a thousand years old.
Later, after the fallen feathers are picked up
we go about our warm partings around the fire,
the social dance, intricate, immortal.

PRAYERS

I eat nothing
and climb Copper Mountain.
Up through debris of old camps,
a three legged chair,
denim with grass growing through,
rakish, rusted springs
– old loneliness, old fucks.
I come out and see woods over the meadow.

Up, through current bush and hemlock,
feet slipping back
skinning green stalks
on small rocks,
I climb to be with someone
a thousand miles away.
On the left a drum of sun
in the dark leaves.
I sidestep over,
clear one small branch,
and sink in,
playing into the instrument.

I begin my prayers like scales,
call to each direction
to strengthen this Dancer
who faces the Sun
for four days without water.
Rich inwardness of the West
strengthen her ankles
dancing out of the body into vision,
North, strength of the big trees,
see forward, forward,
to the East, Spirit, grip
her wrists, draw her
around the circle
even to the South, families,
big heart, beat deep.
Grandfather, sustain her in your power,
Mother, rest her at night.
I see my friend,
the fringes just swaying
as her feet lift and fall softly.

Instead of tobacco
I put sage on the ground,
the gray-green desert color
different from the wood's leaves around,
as my skin is different
whatever my heart
not the People's copperness.
I relax back into the ground.
As in love, there is no skin between us,
my belly is the duff, my arms
sticks and rocks
that are soft with dark dampness.
My sweat dry, the flies
no longer sip at me. I see
a beetle climbing a tree,
a black note moving
on the staff of the brush.
One chickadee brings two others,
nervous, to look at me
and sing territory, territory.

Every place one goes
– as the immigrants found –
is someone else's.
Had my grandfather stayed in Wales
I would now be thick as coal,
steel of the mills,
an owner's daughter.
I roll to my other side
and doze. Sukuyb'Tet,
we're dancing. My love
shawls you as at social dances.
I am the silken fringe that sways,
the arch in your eyebrows.

Afternoon clouds sprinkle lightly,
blessing with a little cool rain.
The greens all around me
– leaves of current, aspen, false Solomon's seal –
smell powerfully astringent,
noticeable now because in childhood
I was half green myself.
There is an aspen propping me,
and one at my feet
rising like a pale green river
crossed by delicate ledges.

It runs into leaves a great distance,
landscape in a landscape.
Now, just before dark,
I pray for all the pain
– the destitute, the abandoned.
addicts, Indian families, mine,
and her endurance of the Sun –
landscape in a landscape.
Whether or not I fit in depends.
I fluff up the ground, straighten
the little branches, turn over pale leaves.
I have been here but only an Indian would know.

THE OLD ONES
a spirit journey

On Chakra mesa
above the stone cities
in Chaco Canyon
I walk a straight road
of packed dirt and bedrock
curbed seven hundred years ago.
We are the ground we walk on
the Pueblos say today.
Cicadas sing in the sun
and my canteen tastes of clay.

I have been here all my life,
walking towards a gate
in superb masonry.
I can imagine other lands
but I walk the desert patiently.
The poems have moved back and forth
like traders, east and west,
words carrying the goods,
but I am illusion
in this heat intense as sex.

The gate nears,
a keyhole of blue in a black wall,
broader above the waist,
for burdens perhaps
– everything was carried on the back.
I see the Spirit in things
on its other side,
lightness, balance,
feel them fit, perhaps, in me.

But my vision is blocked
by two serpents
churning as one.
They stop, knotted together,
and I question them.
Their name is my parents' untrustworthiness.
They have their lesson,
to not be naive.

A hawk spirals. What does she see
of us, frozen in confrontation?
The gate is only in some ruins
but my life has led to it.

LAKOTA PRAYERS FOR LOIE AT 4 PM

It's the garbage
in the air, water, dirt, food,
particles of contamination
in us, at all ages now,
in all places, but especially
the generative organs, breasts, testes,
especially the breasts. We are not to reproduce,
says the garbage-laden earth,
we are too many, that's what's done it,
this lump in your breast over your heart.

Tunkashila, hold Loie's substance
in respect so that we may care for her
as she cares for others, prays
for the cleansing of the earth,
prays for care to return.
Waken Tanka, Maka,
hold her carefully as a child.

Doctors, do your best
and hear our souls.
Prayers are old, old Medicine,
bonds with the spirit,
with all our relations.
Tunkashila, Wakan Tanka,
guide Loie on this journey.
Maka, relent!
Ho, mitakuye iyasin.

FIRST HEALING CEREMONY

Over a year
opening, examining the self,
strengthening, becoming deliberate,
feeling wilder.
Tonight I smudge space
around a patient and myself,
clean and strengthen the air with sage, cedar,
pass the bundle's smoke
over my eyes to see carefully,
ears to hear carefully, hands
to be careful, heart to feel carefully,
around my head for care-full thoughts,
my feet to walk the red road carefully.
Then I pass smoke over her eyes to see calmly,
ears to hear calmly,
mouth to speak calmly, hands
calm, calm feelings,
calm thoughts, calm way of going,
for she has come to me with pain
knotted in her center,
where the duodenum would be.

She is thirty, has two children, a bad marriage.
I begin to teach her how to breathe deeply,
rhythmically, in and out to a count,
the breaths abdominal, large and easy,
in the nose, out the mouth.
Then I light a candle
and have her concentrate on a thought
she'd like to get out, get rid of,
and breathe out the candle with it.
I light it again,
for a feeling,
for a spiritual block,
and last, for a physical sensation,
perhaps the pain, breathed out, out.
Sometimes it takes her several breaths
but pain snuffs the flame instantly.
Then I teach her
to relax, slowly, from feet to crown.
I smudge her again with sage
and feather, brushing off the last tension,
especially just below the sternum,
and offer thanks
to Great Spirit for this good day,
for this ceremony.

34

DOCTORING

Molecules of sound
fly from the rattle into the muscle
among its fibers, releasing
tension that is pain.
The arm shifted the car this morning.
This is as true as aspirin.
Centuries of rational, scientific men
are in my blood
but if I let go and circle myself
in concentration,
focus in the heart of sound,
see into suffering
better than can machinery,
something can be done.

EARTH DAY DAWN, 1990

A few of us walk out across the dump.
It is covered with a thin skin of dirt,
grass and birds,
little trees, weeds, some stone circles.
Earth-making out of garbage.
The air is heady with methane.

We bring sage
and keep smudging,
smoke thick in the wind.
Circling near trees
among yellow boulders,
we begin prayers
for Mother Earth,
gratitude for water, dirt,
fire, and all the creatures,
for the ground we stand on,
the wind.

We are Native American, black,
some white, Saliel
whose jungles in Brazil
are burning.
This prophesied time! The drum
begins, we sing,
redwing blackbirds sing.

Four spiders
come from the stones.
A marsh hawk hunts in the dawn,
harassed by sparrows.
The new little tree
where we hang prayer ties
is more urgent than christmas.

THE LONGEST LIGHT
Summer Solstice

Waves of green
push out into the water,
clumps of grasses, bushes,
the pickleweed,
the light.

Having left the group
that walks the other shore in a pack,
I am sad for them,
for my isolation,
for the river between us.

The bufflehead leads
her ducklings on a silver string
into this longest evening.
The black-necked stilt
frets as her chicks come out
of the grasses dipping, dipping,
and unconcerned.

My sadness slows me down,
walking carefully over the mud,
brush at my ankles,
my heart full of prayers.

When I get to the silver log
the glinting grasses blur.
A shore bird sings in the channels.
Mother Earth, in your summer fullness,
the light doesn't let go
easily. It is eight thirty
and the sun rests on heavy fog
coming over the hills
as slowly as glaciers.

III – DREAM WORK

BACK OF THE DUMP

Bright silver,
terns, like forks,
are plunging into the water.
Their food is evasive.

It is evening-coming-on,
wide sky filled with worn jet trails.
On the bleak gravel road
bicyclists lift through the fence barrier,
and I walk as slowly as the hour.

I could not go inside tonight
though three fishermen say hello,
their friendliness
not friendly,

but I couldn't go inside.
Beginning counsel with you,
you giving me back my feelings,
my loneliness,

I am sustained as the terns fishing
the incoming tide,
their tails tines, pointing
wings forward
over slow water.

LATE COUNSEL

The first skill
is to love the sufferer, draw out the pain
by the intensity of your knowledge of it.
I look up and your eyes
are crying for me.

I am old and used to my hurt,
you are still sensitive.
I want to follow you
but if I cry
it will not be for medicine;
only for love,
for arms around me,

and this little distance
between our chairs
is that between elements,
the spark flying between us
– close the gap
and there is no light –
but no one
has ever cried for me.

FOUNDATIONS

The Connecticut woods are filling up
with rich new houses and snow.
I can't stand the holiday tension
and walk out
of my mother's house.
What am I come here to learn?
The brook is frozen under
and I mutter to it
that blood is thicker than intelligence.
The dried weeds
rattle their exquisite patterns
around the old cellar holes,
seeds hooking in my bootlaces.
With cold fingers I pick them out.
Walking down the powerlines,
the path there clear,
a deer the color of bark
walks along the trees with me.
She is articulated branches,
she is my heart.

ELEVEN YEARS OLD

I watch the family move
in its walls
that are papered over.
The country menage,
sun, gardens, books, animals,
but no honest talk.
And conversation is the point,
isn't it?
Saying who we are,
the wit of our recognitions?
It takes courage.

Animals took all the feeling.
I cried on my horse's neck,
my brother loved a chicken,
hunting dogs were my father's companions,
my mother's confidant, her spaniel.
My father and I cut cedar,
pulled the roots
clearing the view,
but after, high tea
before the fireplace,
there was only relentless chat.

SCHOOL

Dust. I was writing in dust
with an eraser,
curses, swear words,
nine years old.
A playground
but what desperate business –
the kids' meanness,
my parents hatred of each other,
isolation I lived in.

The tears will not come again
though I write and write.
Then someone pushes
my back
and I fall forward
onto the pencil point.
It pierces my hand.
I am crucified on my own wickedness.

The strict principal will see
the filth I write, she
will beat me. My tears pour,
I scream, and they bring me
to her quiet office.
I think she pulled the pencil out.
I have no scar.
Did I imagine all my stigmas?

HUNTING SKETCHES

I

There is something gentle in his hunter's clothes,
a smell of canvas and the corduroy collar,
the game pocket's dried blood salty as kelp.
How did his hands smell handling the birds,
the partridge, pheasant, quail, limp on his bench
in a great pile, my brother stroking them?
We were taught to handle guns very early.
Protection, they said, like learning to swim.
And what if there had been no weapons?
They had been what drew him and his father together,
long fall trips in the Maine woods,
now a little easy hunting in Connecticut,
and not as satisfying, though with his only friend.
My father missed his father who'd killed himself.
He handled guns, killed, to remember
because he really had nothing against animals.
He treated his dogs very lovingly, loved birds,
taught me the names of all the ducks
and painted each feather painstakingly
on the cork-bodied decoy heads.
Look, he said, they're thickest around the eye.
He wanted me to see through his metaphor,
I know he did, so hunting didn't entirely disgust me,
this elegant slaughter by the aristocracy.

II

The reeds smell of mussel shells and mud
and as he plucks them
to camouflage the boat
they whisper again.
Sky is blind and dark
and I, the hunter's child, am cold.
We push off, the dog sitting on the duckboards.
The gun lies in its case, lead circles
hang around the decoys' necks
light streams up from the edge of the Sound.
He throws the decoys into a clear space.
There is no softness, no sound.
He has forgotten his tenderness in bringing me.
Golden eye finally flew in.
He banged away at them, bloodying the dawn.
I held him responsible for everything.

III

After upland shooting in October
we'd come back to the house at dusk
smelling of fallen leaves and dead grasses.
The dogs had an enormous supper
and we took warm baths.
Then my father stretched out on his bed,
damp and naked, and had me massage him,
usually on his back, but then
sometimes he'd roll over
and I'd rub him all around
that hypnotizing penis,
never touching it.
I don't know how old I was,
probably between seven and twelve,
because later I remember
him having to give my brother and me quarters
to do it. It never stopped
because when my daughter was three
he began it all over again. I had forgotten
the whole thing but this time
he had her jerk him off.
If I'd been there, found out, I would have shot him.

DANCING WITH MY BROTHER

It was after another funeral.
The love of mother's life
lay in the living room
for days.
Finally services were done
and my brother and I
took off with his ex-wife and my daughter
and went to New Haven.
The ballrooms glittered,
light spheres spun,
colors sprinkling over us
like autumn leaves.
The sleaze was delicious
as icy drinks.
Getting drunker
we drove from palace to palace
and flung our arms and legs
next to each other in rhythm.
This was not my wedding
when I was in an ivory gown
and we waltzed gingerly.
That was also fantasy.
Coming from our family
there were no marriages possible.
We could not even love each other very well
but dancing
was some relief.

MORNING ANALYSIS

The back-up bell of the bulldozer
down in the meadow
tearing up the earth
is bitter as the wrangling birds
defending their nest.
The jay flies off screaming.

I feel as raw as dirt
and shocked rocks scattered about,
as torn open as the junco eggs,
my long, old life, shell fragments.
Waking is violent, cries out
that exposure
is what is killing the earth,

but there is no closing the ground
over knowing, now,
that I dug my own traps.
Though I lay twigs and moss over them, gently,
it was to catch occasions for grief
that I could not grieve
when I was a child.

Forests can be replanted, mines
filled, grasses left alone,
but I cannot restore my ignorance.
I have set up tragedies,
caused pain, fierce as any jay
out foraging. The psyche is a pirate
of all that resembles
its first experience
and calls it love.

BREAKTHROUGH

Today I suffer
my childhood,
the horrendous fear
that they'd kill each other,
that I caused it,
that I'm abandoned.

Waves and waves of fear.
I am a beach gouged out,
caves cut into me,
crumbled cliffs,
sweat soaks me every few minutes.

I am the red-tailed hawk
hanging in the updraft
watching my shadow
on small animals that freeze,
little teasing birds,
a raven walking.

I am the quiet wind
that dries the sweat,
the breath of speaking out.
The sand seethes
as the tide pulls back.

GO DOWN

Go down to the riverbank and join tears. Water
will carry past feelings you have no permission for,
the wavelets soak them with light. There, sit still, sufferer.

The steel shadows of the rapids, cutlasses at each rock.
The alders, elders I sit among, water ouzel
at my feet, bird on a stone in a thumbprint of ripples.

The lovers got into the car to take their preoccupation to a picnic
where I don't want to go because I can't play softball any more,
a bad arm. The shame of pain, the violent fear of its exposure.

We are animals living by our strengths – legs, arms, sex, teeth.
If we can no longer crouch and spring we will starve.
If we expose our pain the tribe will abandon us.

I go off alone before that can happen. The dark shadow under the rocks
is also the dark blue between the clouds. Elder alders, old, old bush,
I will not abandon you. As a kid I got to watersides through you.

And here we are again, your new leaves soft as babies' tongues.
A robin haunts the other shore as though the river were its lawn.
I do not smell the water till I face upstream. The smell is moss and brown.

The alder branches all crook at fanciful angles, no branch
thicker than a penis, some of the dark, leathery leaves eaten into lace.
When we get older we include both genders unless we get very artificial.

Grandfather, it's to you I appeal for warmth, Grandmother, you are stern
with the truth. Uncle Leonard, I'm afraid of your Sundance the sweats
will be so hot. They will show me I can't stand much. Exposed. Weakness.

You can't stand it? Shame, shame. A movement in my bowels.
Must I leave or can I find a place to bury myself?
Under a spruce in loose duff. Wiped with mule ear leaves. Soft.

Coming back to the river thinking of elders, that when they die
we carry their responsibility, and that I feel strong enough,
but that I will miss them so much, even my mother who's harsh.

50

Mother earth, whose horsetail and sedge I sit among,
whose mosquitos search my arms, even my breast,
your waterbugs are partying by this rock.

Each time two approach each other, at a certain distance
they rebound, negative magnetism. My closest love,
you are three thousand miles away. Is our magnetism that strong?

There are two spruce cones in the sedge by my thigh,
nestled together like a pair of mice, little lovers, the whorl of the scales
like the thumbprint current under the waterbugs. Related. All my relations.

MY WAYS

I take my sharpest knife, a sack, and climb the mountain
into a meadow of sage. Where else would I be able to harvest this year?
Without the red-wound bundles it is hard to pray,
I come to prayer distracted, and smelling of distraction,
and the smudge washes me in the breath of the earth
whose smoke is more searching than water.

The plants spring up like light, silvery leaves little ears along the woody stem.
I find a Grandmother plant, full and flourishing,
ask her if it is alright to harvest some, these are dry years.
Yes, she says, if you take a fifth instead of a third, and step carefully.
I thank her, leave leaves of my own at her base, do not touch her,
and go off cutting the highest spears. The smell in the sack is overwhelming.
When I try to cut lower, a careless, grabbing handful,
I slip and cut my knuckle on a rock.

There is so much healing to be done.
Most nights I cannot sleep without prayer and the smudge,
often the analysis, crucial to my life now, nearly destroys me,
all the stuctures of my life at my feet like a devastated plant,
stems torn, leaves slashed. A mountainside of ravaged life
as though bulldozers had been at it to make condominiums.

New life will come but the old natural connections are broken –
trees, streams, grasses, and the horrendous cycles of family life.
Before ceremony one purifies, the sage leading prayers, dances.
These ways can heal, can heal us, the spirit leading us out of confusion.
And the construction worker, smudging the cab of his truck as I do my car?
Only if he's Washoe. And then what does it mean? That he's safe?

These days I see injury everywhere, in others, myself, the earth. I light
the bundle and fan the smoke over my head for clear thoughts, over eyes
for clear sight, ears to hear clearly, mouth to speak without cloudiness, down
over the heart for clear feelings, around the body clockwise for the whole self,
and down the legs to the feet, that they walk the good road clearly.
Once around the hands. Then such peacefulness. This life takes much Medicine.

PROGRESS

Climbing, searching for footfall among mule ears, thistle, stones,
the back-up bells like my ringing breaths,
all I really saw were the spruce and fir I headed for.
I was getting away. High enough for perspective, I turned, and there
– defying trees, cliff, river, the earth itself – a black-windowed hotel
and stupid little ponds the bulldozers dug, the entire landscape.

I had wanted to study the root at my feet, end of an immense log,
history so old it was folding into the ground. That's what lay before me.
I labored up under the perilous light, risking my skin,
but turned, like Lot's wife, and stood in my drying sweat.
Two ravens launched above my head and croaked into the valley
but they were driven back by the dust
from scraping machines, Tonka toy trucks driven by men.

Coming down it matters so much. I ignore the flowers.
Sitting on the rock to shake out pebbles, I don't smell the grasses.
I lose paradise from the spoiled land and from my fury.
Coming into the patch of silver sage, I want to cut it,
take it all home. Even harvested sacredly,
taking only a third and offering prayers, there isn't enough.
I will eat up the earth, the ground I stand on. I haven't learned.
I return to the study of my past. There is no other way
until I understand why I would rather destroy than love my life.

SABOTAGE

Throwing a sabot into the machinery,
1870, or the Luddites in England burning the mills
as I nearly burned down a school
– all so things would not move ahead
without care for the people involved.
A shoe, wooden, obstructive,
in the door –
listen to me!

That's what my psyche does,
takes off its shoes
and hurls them into my ventures.
The great, wooden machinery of happiness
stops so abruptly I'm thrown
as though from a lever
and flung to the ground,
unconscious.

Maybe
that's why
my unconscious
throws things, to make me
senseless. What
would happiness reveal?
You brush your hand on my cheek,
I say something subtle, wounding.
You leave.

If I allowed myself to be pleased
I would find out
how I hate to be left,
how I want your hand there, now.
By now I am too old and fat
to be desired.
I have finally achieved
exactly what my psyche allows.

It has fallen so far,
like a monkey wrench into a turbine,
that even the spring sun makes me sad.
Happiness being unbearable
I've only really loved
the edge of air that cuts off the leaves
and bleeds them into winter.

DREAM WORK

I do not take the dream seriously enough,
that those who move through it,
in apparent integrity, are my selves.
So many people in this small room,
as you say there were six of us in bed
after marriage, all the parents
we thought we had married each other to lose.

The masks on the wall grin, ceremonially,
from all over the world. We are one.
And the hawk, and the drum.
This is now the ceremony. I bring you
a lot of money, enough for you to live on,
as I would bring you tobacco,
and you listen as a Medicine person would.
In the dream there is a flood, a marriage, a dog,
two psychiatrists and an artist.

Your glasses are crystal, light
bounces from them. I am hypnotized.
What do you see? You take the glasses off,
rub your lids and nose – heaviness.
You have cried for sadness,
there have been tears of anger, of laughter.
You are living me. It is your magic.
No lover could go deeper.

I sit on a small couch, cannot see the clock,
but you begin to get restless, shift.
Here, just here, on this perimeter, stop.
I do not want to leave, where,
for once, I am satisfied as at a meal
that feeds actual hunger,
which is – to be known.

Shape-shifter, all the faces in me,
you finally convince me, are mine.
The gay lover I leave, following
the spirited dog, is me, the faithless lover
is me, the artist whose studio is too small
because he has so many friends, is me, the painter's wife,
cheerful in the background, is me, what bubbles up
through the floor is my consciousness,
I am the unknown girl who's getting married.

I come from a family of suicides.
I am at least half dead, and waking,
dear heart, I tell you
I will not move from this place
though my house is taken from me.
I will find any shack to stay
in this vicinity till the foundations are set,
the new cement seasoned. I will not move away!
For as you are all others to me, as you
are all selves in me, we are also each other,
and I will not abandon my self any more.

Perhaps I pay you to not be sexual,
a kind of reverse prostitution,
though it is intimacy I'm seeking,
that I walk the streets of my dreams for.
What comes out of the shadows is knowledge.
Myself at two years old sitting on the back step
looking at the food the dogs are given, the attention,
not sure I want to live.

BODY WORK

This body is the house they whisper in,
especially as the abdomen
is loosened, straightened, opened,
their voices are magnified in there
though they never call out,
argue, drink, fight,
my organs are their instruments,
keyboard, drum, thumbscrew.
Between all my bones
the juices of their voices
dry up and scrape.

I had no anger
but a tension that twisted my torso
as surely as my uncle's poor body walked sideways.
His intelligent humor couldn't save him,
he'd wear no brace,
but bravely loved beautiful, wraithlike young men.

As you bring me around,
with light pressure, counter pressures
skillful as love, perhaps
now there is room for me to inhabit myself.
When you free the ovaries
I cry for more babies
my clumsiness denied me.
Tears, so many tears, many
as sperm that never reached me.

Going the long way home, my body
is not like my old body
that belonged to others
but my own, turning at signals,
flying over the wheels
like eagle, crow, heron,
lifting to speak to Spirit,
or resting in the trees like leaves.

OPERA

I woke about five,
the light slow, dim,
slow, dim, thick
as the Prelude
to *Tristan*.
It deepened
into grief.

I treat my life
with the same distance
my parents did me.
They were not
three thousand miles
off, they stood
between me and myself.

I mourned
and mourned
the lost closeness
as Isolde
mourned her lover.
I got up and left
before it was done,
like a suburban audience,
but I have begun.

IV – BREATH

CROSSING LONG ISLAND SOUND

The water wipes back from the fat bow
in quiet rows
and it has a flat sound.
You would not know there are bass
embedded under the wash,
crabs near the inlet bridges.
Nothing should live today,
least of all yourself, you feel,
but say to my mother, We go on, we go on,
and close your lapels against the wind.
Gulls cried for you, cried
as the ferry bumped out of its slip
and a child threw them morsels of bread.
O Charon, this man's son has died,
let him pass.
The three stacks of Port Jefferson
rise above and my mother's hand
takes your elbow to the car.
You sit in it, wait. Docked,
it seems to drive itself
to the terrible shore.

LESSONS

Gloves, scarves, coats – thrown on a chair.
Your teacher's husband comes out,
greets me as though he loves you.
You make me tea in the little kitchen
and I settle on the apartment couch,
European paintings as warm as brandy
over my head, no rug at my feet.
No one is at the piano, the teacher sits beside it,
and you stand facing a bookcase
of her scores and photographs of young singers.
Your legs tense as though you face an army.
There is no warm-up, no accompaniment,
and Isolde begins.

I sit still, later make cautious remarks.
Your teacher, singing very low with you
sometimes, murmurs, Again,
more forward, not behind the cheeks.
You stop, repeat.
Outside the gray New York rain
dances around the building
flickering the lights, your powerful voice
blowing out the walls into the street.
You are not shrill but the third day,
for the first time, I hear your voice trying.
Your teacher, her husband, are exhausted.

They say, my daughter, that you have everything,
will be a diva, magnificent, the best.
I am not used to these absolutes.
No words about music
work, but when, as your voice opens and soars,
your hand reaches out,
I want to take it.

THE HEIGHTS

On the highest rock in New York
we sit in a drift of locust petals
and talk about how to live.
What you propose for friendship
I have always known as love.

Behind us kids play ball, skate,
the old sun and chat
and your dog rests in my lap like a child.
Finally your arm is around my shoulders,
the sense of sitting within you
powerful as intercourse.

In the new living room
with both your daughters
we sprawl and talk of their school plans,
argue a little.
I have not been this peaceful
in twenty years.

Full of afternoon light
you and I chop broccoli,
cut the chicken, set out plates,
and arrange our meal together.
Haven't we always done this?

When the city gets dark
we play sonatas as others make love,
the music bedrock:
Mozart, Dvôrák, Schubert.

THE HEALERS

> *And in this consumation, all withheld*
> *Except the soul upon a shining field.*
>   May Sarton

I

Ocean breaks up out of itself
green, lavender in shadow,
silver all else.
The light is pulled from us,
beloved, out of our bellies.

A red-tailed hawk above the cliff
holds motionless,
god's eye.
Will we do anything important with each other?
My hand strokes your chest
round and round its shield,
warms it, opens location. Here
is the awful pain,
the isolation.
Sun holds us in this hollow,
logs blocking the wind.

Walking through long kelp, later,
I whip the sand.
Your laugh is small. Beloved,
the hawk is looking at your heart.
Divided from women, perhaps,
in first desire, intense as a fuse,
you burned away from her,
and then wounded, she wounded you.

II

You thought I was a cellist
because I resonate so for you.
I tune the smaller violin,
how I made my living
work.
As you begin to warm up at the piano
I hear the lightness
in your hands.
Before we talk much about it,
ecstatic, grabbing notes,
gluing our phrases together,
we are playing,

III

Out in the baylands,
pickleweed and power stanchions,
noisy, at moments, with small planes,
we walk through some brow-beaten children.
We slip through their small bodies,
the awful voice – do this, do that –
I stroke the last one's frail shoulder.
Once through
we hold tightly to each other,
hands glued. I take you
out through the mud, the bushes,
lead you out along water
very far away.
Here we mount a warm log,
you behind me, face on my shoulder,
and we ride together into silence.
The marsh is so still
that when whimbrels come
we hear their feathers.

MENOPAUSE

I

This blood
ties and unties
through every tissue.
I see it in your older temple
and I feel it up my arm
as you describe meridians
like a chart of arteries.
This point to this point to this.
I count days like stitches between periods
now that they soon will stop.

Ah damn that little death.
The thread of blood
will tie itself into knots
as I twist the sheets
dreaming I have been condemned.
This change
pulls all change with it.

The torso shudders as though with flu,
breasts hot and sore
as though more were coming
but nothing comes.
The thermostat is off
and I overheat, stalled.

II

There is traffic in the trees,
susurrus of boughs on the mountain.
My attention draws down
– the low branches old and silver –
to a perfect drypoint of the vascular system.
I stand before it as at a museum,
cool, analyzing its form,
until a small animal I can't see
whimpers.

This pulling in
knits me deeper into life,
shrinking me
until I'm dense as felt
with intelligence of the physical.

Tonight, up between the sugar pines,
the constellation
that is wisdom, the archer,
draws the the bow that is our blood,
propelling us into the stars.

III

We go nowhere without ourselves,
without limbs and breath, muscle
and menstrual cycle. Not even to the moon.
Too often I try to be detached,
impatient at the push of hormones.
Then I am no better than the engineer
who thinks his way to missiles.

We go nowhere without ourselves
and therefore without each other.
My husband and daughter invented a game
played on a board like chess
for long evenings in winter
when the trees cracked at zero.
To win you had to bring
your adversary with you.

I am a terrible example, a solitary.
I listen to the river at night
at the end of the meadow
as though the moon in the shallows
were my only familiar.
Blood ties me to her, to my daughter,
the onslaught of winter.

BREATH

Breath, count the breaths,
                    this will lead
to nothing, detachment. That is all
that wisdom requires. Since I've been fourteen
I've wanted to be wise and thought it would fill me up
but wisdom empties.
                My friend, as you pack your mother's things
to be sold now, she is so old she gives up all control:
bladder, bones, possessions. O Marguerite, you are the future.
Anything we have is only to use for a while,
there are few generations to inherit anymore.
                      Family
is chance now, and the generations must begin alone.
Do not investigate this. Wretchedness.
Clarity brings me to wretchedness.
                    Breathe.
Breathe in acceptance, breathe out action. Female, male,
the genders again. My strangest fantasy is that I'm a homosexual man,
a man-loving boy as my father brought me up to be his companion.
I am also female.
              The mystery of sex to me
is that I felt no one ever really wanted it with me very much.
The strong female frightening men is not enough to explain it.
When a new friend expounded on love, I shriveled up,
froze in utter wretchedness.
                Once I thought about love, thought
I had ideas about it, thought it was central to my being.
Now I know nothing. Breathe, breathe again.
                    Count the breaths,
they are not endless. Death is not that far; perhaps in a thief's knife.
I see that I am not immortal and that my poems may fail.
I begin to come close to Spirit.
                  Old women
who pray are a hated caricature in our culture,
though Native Americans love old women, value their wisdom,
will even sleep with them, at least one lover did.
                    Breathe,
I have lost him too, the best, the freest. Sleep is very peaceful now

though last night I did dream of being in an earthquake,
standing beside my bed, going for the door frame.
                                        I'm going on
like an old woman. How old women are despised! Why? Even I
stopped visiting Marguerite because she went on about you,
her son, so badly.
                        She is so old, so alone, and now in a nursing home.
My own mother's changed and seems to want to acknowledge me,
even love me.
                It utterly confuses me. I am based
on not being loved. Breathe, count the breaths, it is nothing.

"SELF PORTRAIT OF THE OTHER"

Herberto Padilla's guards beat him
while reciting his lines,
threw him about the room to their rhythms,
from wall to wall, to the floor,
into their fists and kicks,
extreme payment for being one's self out loud.
It is that dangerous.
If only our poets knew
that it matters.
We suffer from being ignored,
the dismissed, the utterly non-present
to what concerns most people.
You have to be rich to be taught from books.
Padilla said his suffering was strange,
felt almost random,
except to protect a power
had no purpose.

A LOVE POEM

He was just stepping out of my car,
putting something in his pocket.
Bulging with bags of groceries,
I go right up to him near the tail light
and say, "Huh, hey, what are you doing?"
The universal stupid question.
He holds his ground under my glare,
a head shorter, brown, his eyes snapping and puzzled,
"I didn't do nothing." Big, gray-haired, white,
I lean closer. "Did you take anything?"
"I not take nothing." I believe him
and look deeper in his eyes.
Pain like light, intense pain.
Liquor he drank to get up his courage
fumes from him like his shivers
in the cold night.
I make a strange gesture with my hand
and turn back to the car. Nothing
is gone – my sack of manuscripts,
a priceless olivera shell necklace,
tapes of chants, the feather.
The air's a bit alcoholic but I turn the key.
A while later, turning on the radio,
it almost falls into my hand
and I think, I bet he's thinking
"I almost take something."
What was in his pocket was a screwdriver,
neither gun nor knife I was afraid
my question would bring out.
Probably no papers,
no job, and the door was open. That night
I pray to the six directions for him.

WRITING ON GLASS

In October the bees in the scarlet salvia
drill with the humming birds.
How is their industry
different from ours?
When is hunger supportable?
The red spires shake with assault.

This is written on glass
that curves around the screen.
Will it hold longer
than the clicks of the keys
faster and softer than typewriters,
easier to erase than pencil?

How can a poem hold still, hold us still?
As I read to a room full of engineers
there is such stillness
as though they hear the danger they are
though what they say they hear
is earth, air, fire, water.

Under the acid rain the spruce
become forests of red spires.
No birds will come to them.
There are fewer birds.
Fish in the lake float
like a hoard of arrowpoints
washed up on the margin.

At lunch a steam shovel eats a tree
below the company patio
making room for more and more people.
The bucket opens its jaws
and rips out great mouthfuls of branches.

The earth is about to shrug:
the floods, earthquakes, volcanos,
as necessary as death.
There was a balance point.
To find it watch the bees
sucking up nectar, spreading pollen.

DATE DUE
